NATIONAL GEOGRAPHIC

Why Did They Come?

Solomon Gordon

Millions of people came to the United States in the 1800s. They arrived from places all over the world. Why did they come?

People who came to the United States in the 1800s came on ships. Most of them arrived in New York.

Some people came because they didn't have enough to eat. People came from Ireland because the potato crop was not safe to eat. There wasn't enough food for people in Ireland in the 1840s.

Irish families relied on their potato crops for food.

Some people came to make money. People came from Europe to find jobs in factories. Many factories opened in the United States in the 1850s.

Many factory workers came from Europe.

Some people came looking for work. People came from China to work on the railroads. Rail lines were built across the country in the 1860s.

Many Chinese people helped build the railroad tracks that now cross the United States.

Some people came to escape from danger. Jewish people came to escape from Russia. Russia was not a safe place for Jewish people to live in the 1880s.

Jewish people took only what they were able to carry when they escaped from Russia.

11

When did people in your family first come to the United States? Why did they come? What countries did they leave behind?